CORAL REEFS

By Melissa Cole

Photographs By Brandon Cole

BLACKBIRCH®
PRESS

THOMSON

GALE

San Diego • Detroit • New York • San Francisco • Cleveland • New Haven, Conn. • Waterville, Maine • London • Munich

For more information, contact
The Gale Group, Inc.
27500 Drake Rd.
Farmington Hills, MI 48331-3535
Or you can visit our Internet site at http://www.gale.com

Photo Credits: Cover, all photos © Brandon D. Cole; illustrations by Chris Jouan Illustration

LIBRARY OF CONGRESS CATALOGING-IN-PUBLICATION DATA

Cole, Melissa S.
  Coral reefs / by Melissa S. Cole.
    p. cm. — (Wild marine habitats)
Summary: Discusses what coral reefs are, what makes them unique, where they are found, what plants and animals make up their food webs, and what impact humans have on these fragile ecosystems.
Includes bibliographical references and index.
  ISBN 1-56711-908-5 (hardback : alk. paper)
  1. Coral reef ecology—Juvenile literature. 2. Coral reefs and islands—Juvenile literature. [1. Coral reef ecology. 2. Coral reefs and islands. 3. Coral reef animals. 4. Ecology.]
I. Title II. Series: Cole, Melissa S. Wild marine habitats.

  QH541.5.C7C55 2004
  578.7789—dc21   2003010090

Printed in United States
10 9 8 7 6 5 4 3 2 1

Contents

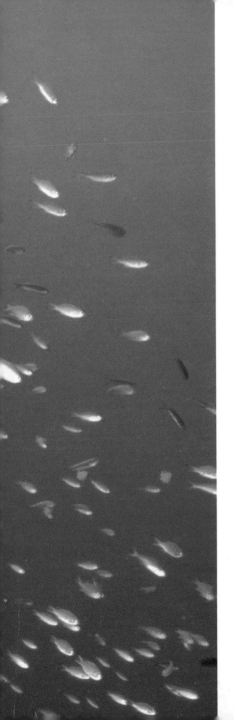

Introduction

A habitat is a place where a group of animals and plants naturally live together. One ocean habitat is the coral reef. A reef is a ridge on the ocean floor. It can be made of sand, rock, or coral. Coral reefs are found in many tropical oceans.

A coral reef looks like a colorful hill rising up from the sandy ocean floor. The outside of the reef is made up of colonies of tiny, tube-shaped creatures called coral polyps. Some kinds of coral polyps protect themselves by growing hard limestone skeletons on the outside of their bodies. The core of the reef is made up of these skeletons. When the coral polyps die, their skeletons pile up, and the reef gets bigger. After thousands of years, coral reefs can become very large.

There are more than 2,500 species of coral polyps, but only 650 build reefs. These corals are called hard corals. Colonies of hard corals can be shaped like antlers, fingers, mounds, or even brains! Corals that cannot build reefs are called soft corals. Colonies of soft corals can be shaped like trees, bushes, flowers, and fans.

Millions of the tiny skeletons of coral polyps make up the core of a coral reef.

Coral reef habitats are found in the warm, shallow water of tropical oceans. They cover more than 80 million square miles (207 million square km) of sea floor. Australia's Great Barrier Reef is the longest coral reef in the world. It is more than 1,250 miles (2,000 km) long.

The coral reefs with the greatest numbers of plant and animal species are found in the Indo-Pacific. This region includes the Indian Ocean, western Pacific Ocean, and the Red Sea. The Indo-Pacific stretches across Hawaii, Indonesia, the Philippines, Egypt, and Australia.

Coral reefs are found in warm, tropical waters all over the world.

Coral reefs are also located off the Florida Keys and around many islands in the Caribbean Sea. There are also reefs in the Pacific Ocean off the west coast of Central and South America.

Coral reefs are unique because they are partly made up of living creatures. Coral reefs are home to many interesting sea creatures and schools of colorful reef fish.

Coral reefs are dependent on the cycles of the moon. After a full moon, corals all over the world spawn, or reproduce, at the same time. Individual polyps release sperm and eggs into the water. The sperm fertilizes the eggs. These eggs hatch into baby polyps that settle on the ocean floor and form new reefs.

Colorful fish and plants make coral reefs their home.

8

Coral reefs need a climate of warm, clear salt water to grow. They are only found in ocean water with temperatures between 75°F. and 85°F. (24°C and 30°C). Corals grow best at shallow depths of 6 to 100 feet (2 to 30 m) because they need sunlight to grow.

Coral reefs need sunlight and warm, clear salt water to grow.

Storms such as hurricanes, cyclones, and typhoons can affect coral reefs. Strong winds and crashing waves can break and damage corals near the surface. Heavy rains can cause temperature changes, muddy water, and too much fresh rainwater. These conditions can destroy coral reefs and their inhabitants.

Strong winds, heavy rain, and crashing waves can damage coral reefs and harm the creatures that live in them.

Algae are the most common plants found on coral reefs. Algae come in many forms. For example, hard algae, called calcareous algae, coat parts of the reef like cement. They hold the coral together and strengthen the reef structure. Seaweed is another form of algae and comes in many shapes and colors. It grows in between clumps of living coral polyps on the reef.

Single-celled algae known as zooxanthellae are the most important plants that live on coral reefs. These plants live inside the hard coral's body tissues. This protects zooxanthellae from plant-eating animals. Like all plants, zooxanthellae create food in the form of sugar by absorbing energy from the sun. In exchange for the coral's protection, the algae share the food they make with the coral. Hard coral polyps use this extra energy to remove minerals such as calcium carbonate from the seawater. Coral polyps need these minerals to form their limestone skeletons and build the hard structure of the coral reef.

Algae such as seaweed (above) and zooxanthellae (below) are the most common plants that grow on coral reefs.

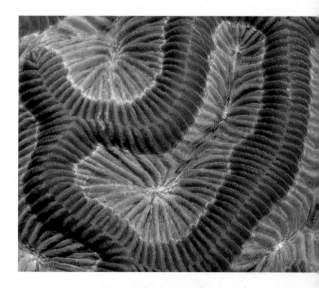

Animals

Coral reefs are home to thousands of different creatures, such as fish, starfish, crabs, and sponges. Each species has its own way of life within the reef habitat. Many have developed special feeding adaptations in order to survive.

Predators are animals that hunt other animals, known as prey, for food. Coral reefs are home to predators such as white-tip reef sharks, barracuda, and jacks. They have adapted to life on the coral reef by resting during the day when their prey is most active. These predators feed mainly at dusk, when many fish are slow and sleepy.

Sea turtles have hard shells and tough skin that protect them from sharks (inset) and other large predators that hunt on coral reefs.

Sea turtles also spend the day resting in caves on the coral reef. Their sharp beaks allow them to spear fish and bite open crabs, shellfish, and sponges. They are protected from most large predators by their hard shells and tough, scaly skin.

Small, colorful predators include trumpet fish, lizard fish, hawk fish, and snappers. These fish use camouflage to hide in their surroundings and catch their prey. For example, a lumpy frog fish can resemble a sponge on a reef. This fish is also known as an anglerfish because it has a special growth on its head shaped like a wriggling worm. When a fish tries to eat the lure, it is quickly swallowed by the waiting frog fish.

Predators like the lumpy frog fish (below) and the reef octopus (opposite) use camouflage to blend into the reef and wait for their prey.

Another small predator is the reef octopus. These amazing creatures can change the color and texture of their skin in an instant. This allows them to crawl along the reef in search of shrimp and crabs without being seen by their enemies.

Other small predators such as cone snails and sea snakes use venom, or poison, to stun their prey. Cone snails use a venomous stinger to kill small fish, worms, and other snails.

In the coral reef habitat, many animals graze, or feed, throughout the day. Butterfly fish and angelfish use their long noses to reach inside cracks in the coral to feed on algae. Triggerfish and parrot fish have big teeth that stick out like a bird's beak. This allows them to munch on the living polyps on the coral reef.

Coral reef creatures including coral polyps, sponges, and tubeworms feed on tiny floating plants and animals known as plankton. These plankton eaters capture tiny bits of food by using feathery gills, tubes, or stinging tentacles.

All corals feed on plankton. Hard corals also gain some energy from their plant partners (zooxanthellae). Unlike hard corals, soft corals do not form limestone skeletons, so they cannot build reefs. Soft corals do not have zooxanthellae living within their tissues, either. These polyps must get all of their energy by feeding directly on plankton.

Some fish use their long noses to feed on algae deep inside cracks in the coral.

Coral polyps feed with a slitlike mouth that takes in plankton and gets rid of wastes. Surrounding the mouth is a ring of stinging tentacles. During the day, coral polyps curl up and rest. At night, they stretch out and use their tentacles to paralyze and then capture bits of plankton in the water.

Anemones are animals that look like upside-down jellyfish. They also live on the reef and use stinging tentacles to capture plankton. Anemones are often home to small, colorful fishes called clown fish or anemone fish. Clown fish have a slippery coating that protects them from the anemone's stinging tentacles.

The colorful clown fish lives among the anemones on the reef.

This allows the fish to hide within the tentacles and be safe from predators. Clown fish help anemones by chasing away butterfly fish, which often feed on anemone tentacles. The anemone may also get extra bits of food when the clown fish feeds.

Certain animals such as banded cleaner shrimp, butterfly fish, gobies, and cleaner wrasses survive by cleaning other animals. Bigger fish line up with their mouths wide open in areas called cleaning stations. The small fish and shrimp pick their teeth, scales, and gills clean. The cleaners get a meal of dead skin and parasites in exchange for their services.

Banded cleaner shrimp (below) and other small creatures feed by cleaning the teeth, scales, and gills of bigger fish (above).

Nothing goes to waste on a coral reef. Animals such as hermit crabs, lobsters, starfish, and worms are important because they keep the reef clean. When an animal dies and sinks to the bottom, these creatures feed on the remains.

Worms are an important part of the coral reef's food chain because they eat the remains of animals that have died and sank to the bottom.

A Coral Reef's Food Chain

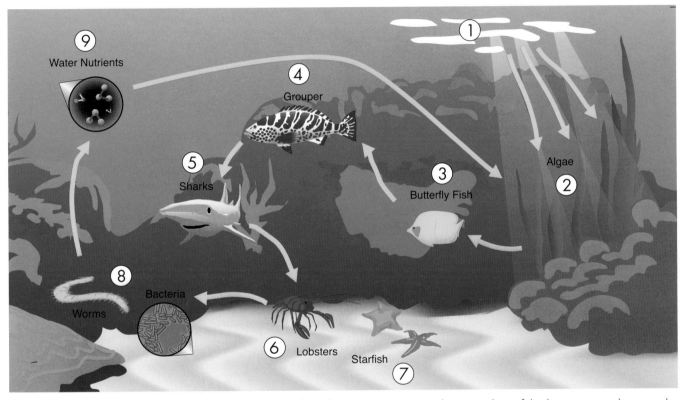

The food chain shows a step-by-step example of how energy in the coral reef habitat is exchanged through food: (1) sunlight is used by (2) algae to make sugar. When a (3) butterfly fish eats the algae, some of the plant's energy becomes part of the fish. When a predator such as a (4) grouper eats the butterfly fish, and a larger predator such as a (5) shark eats the grouper, the energy is passed from creature to creature. When the shark dies, scavengers such as (6) lobsters and (7) starfish feed on the waste. Decomposers such as (8) bacteria and worms break down the last bits until they become part of the sand or mix with seawater. Algae absorbs these (9) nutrients directly from water in addition to the energy it absorbs from the sun. Then the whole cycle begins again.

Humans and Coral Reefs

Coral reefs are important to humans because they act like barriers. In addition, important anticancer medicines are found in corals and sponges.

Coral reefs also provide recreation for scuba divers and snorkelers. People can help preserve coral reefs by not touching coral when they swim.

Modern fishing practices such as traps, nets, poisons, and even dynamite have made fishing easy. These methods of fishing, however, often destroy coral reefs.

Pollution damages coral reefs. When sewage and muddy runoff pour into the ocean after a rain, the particles can clog the pores of the coral.

People can help protect the oceans when they support environmental groups. Some of these groups help pass stricter laws to decrease pollution runoff. This will help ensure a healthy future for coral reefs and their millions of inhabitants.

Nets, traps, dynamite, and other modern fishing practices have destroyed some coral reefs.

A Coral Reef's Food Web

Food webs show how creatures in a habitat depend on one another to survive. The arrows in this drawing show the flow of energy from one creature to another. Yellow arrows: green plants that make food from air and sunlight; green arrows: animals that eat the green plants; orange arrows: predators; red arrows: scavengers and decomposers. These reduce dead bodies to their basic chemicals, which return to the soil to be taken up by green plants, beginning the cycle all over again.

Glossary

Algae Seaweed or one-celled plants that do not have flowers or roots

Anemone A type of marine animal in the same family as coral polyps and jellyfish. It has a tube-shaped body with a mouth surrounded by a ring of stinging tentacles.

Calcareous Algae A type of marine plant that produces minerals such as calcium carbonate. It helps strengthen and cement a coral reef together when it grows.

Cleaning Station A place on the reef where small fish and shrimp clean larger fish; large fish know where these stations are and line up to be cleaned.

Colony A group of animals of the same species, such as coral polyps, that live close together

Coral Polyp The adult stage of the coral animal. It is related to the anemone and is tube-shaped with stinging tentacles.

Limestone A type of rock made of calcium carbonate. Hard coral polyps use limestone to form reefs.

Plankton Tiny floating plants and animals such as young coral, starfish, and crabs that can usually only be seen under a microscope

Predators Animals such as sharks, that hunt other animals for their food

Prey An animal killed and eaten by another animal

Reef A ridge on the ocean floor. A reef can be made of sand, coral, or rock.

Scavengers Animals such as starfish that feed on dead animals

Zooxanthellae Tiny algae plants that live inside the tissues of hard coral polyps and help them build reefs

For More Information

Books

Cerullo, Mary. *Habitats: Coral Reef: A City That Never Sleeps.* Austin: Cobblehill Books, 1996.

Kalman, Bobbie. *Life in the Coral Reef.* New York: Crabtree, 1997.

Sayre, April Pulley. *Coral Reef.* New York: Twenty-First Century Books, 1996.

Web site

www.bir.bham.wednet.edu/Hinshaw/tidepool/tide.htm
This is the "save the tide pool" site of the Birmingham Zoo

Index